W9-DBS-908

Martin Luther King, Jr. Day

Reagan Miller

Crabtree Publishing Company
www.crabtreebooks.com

Crabtree Publishing Company

www.crabtreebooks.com

Author: Reagan Miller
Coordinating editor: Chester Fisher
Series and project editor: Penny Dowdy
Editor: Adrianna Morganelli
Proofreader: Crystal Sikkens
Project editor: Robert Walker
Production coordinator: Katherine Berti
Prepress technician: Katherine Berti
Project manager: Kumar Kunal (Q2AMEDIA)
Art direction: Dibakar Acharjee (Q2AMEDIA)
Cover design: Shweta Nigam (Q2AMEDIA)
Design: Ritu Chopra (Q2AMEDIA)
Photo research: Farheen Aadil (Q2AMEDIA)

Photographs:
Alamy: Dinodia Images: p. 9; Jeff Greenberg: p. 25–26;
  David Grossman: p. 18; F1online digitale Bildagentur GmbH:
  p. 22; North Wind Picture Archives: p. 6; Jim West: p. 20
Corbis: Bob Adelman: p. 1; Bettmann: p. 8, 10–14, 17;
  Raymond Gehman: p. 4; Andrew Lichtenstein/Sygma:
  p. 19; Tom & Dee Ann McCarthy: front cover;
  Flip Schulke: p. 5
Corbis Saba: David Butow: p. 28
Getty Images: Erik S. Lesser/Stringer: p. 21;
  Time & Life Pictures: p. 7
Jupiterimages: p. 29; Leland Bobborbis: p. 27;
  Andersen Ross: p. 24
Photolibrary: Ariel Skelley: p. 31
Reuters: Jonathan Ernst: p. 23
Shutterstock: Taipan Kid: folio glyph; Gianna
  Stadelmyer: p. 30; Katherine Welles: p. 16
Stringer: Barry Williams: p. 15

Library and Archives Canada Cataloguing in Publication

Miller, Reagan
   Martin Luther King, Jr. Day / Reagan Miller.

(Celebrations in my world)
Includes index.
ISBN 978-0-7787-4290-6 (bound).--ISBN 978-0-7787-4308-8 (pbk.)

   1. Martin Luther King, Jr., Day--Juvenile literature. 2. King, Martin
Luther, Jr., 1929-1968--Juvenile literature. I. Title. II. Series: Celebrations
in my world

E185.97.K5 M54 2009   j394.261   C2009-900233-7

Library of Congress Cataloging-in-Publication Data

Miller, Reagan.
   Martin Luther King, Jr. Day / Reagan Miller.
      p. cm. -- (Celebrations in my world)
   Includes index.
   ISBN 978-0-7787-4290-6 (reinforced library binding : alk. paper)
-- ISBN 978-0-7787-4308-8 (pbk. : alk. paper)
   1. Martin Luther King, Jr., Day--Juvenile literature. 2. King, Martin Luther,
Jr., 1929-1968--Juvenile literature. I. Title. II. Series.

   E185.97.K5M496 2009
   394.261--dc22

                                          2009000325

Crabtree Publishing Company

www.crabtreebooks.com   1-800-387-7650

Published in Canada
Crabtree Publishing
616 Welland Ave.
St. Catharines, ON
L2M 5V6

Published in the United States
Crabtree Publishing
PMB16A
350 Fifth Ave., Suite 3308
New York, NY 10118

Published in the United Kingdom
Crabtree Publishing
White Cross Mills
High Town, Lancaster
LA1 4XS

Published in Australia
Crabtree Publishing
386 Mt. Alexander Rd.
Ascot Vale (Melbourne)
VIC 3032

Contents

A U.S. Holiday

Martin Luther King, Jr. Day **honors** the life of Dr. Martin Luther King Jr. King was a brave man. He worked hard to help make the United States a better country.

On Martin Luther King, Jr. Day, flags are flown to show respect for the **civil rights** leader.

DID YOU KNOW?

*Martin Luther King, Jr. Day is a **federal** holiday. Across the country schools, banks, and government offices are closed on federal holidays.*

King believed that all people should be treated equally. He wanted people to stand up for their civil rights.

On this holiday, people remember King's message of **equality** and freedom. People celebrate Martin Luther King, Jr. Day on the third Monday in January. The holiday is always close to King's birthday— January 15.

• Martin Luther King, Jr. helped all Americans gain equal rights.

5

A Journey Back in Time

Hundreds of years ago, people **kidnapped** Africans from their homes. The kidnappers sold the Africans as **slaves** in the United States. Slaves had no **rights** or freedoms. Slave owners forced slaves to work long hours and treated them badly.

- Slaves were forced to work without pay.

DID YOU KNOW?

In some states, African Americans had to use separate water fountains and sit in separate areas on buses. They were not allowed to share with white Americans.

This slavery ended in 1865. Even then, African Americans did not have the same rights as white people in the U.S. Some states passed laws to create **segregation**.

These laws forced African Americans to live separately from white people. African Americans could live, work, and go to church only with other African Americans.

African American children and white children were forced to go to separate schools.

Growing Up

Martin Luther King, Jr. was born on January 15, 1929. He was born and raised in Atlanta, Georgia. King grew up with segregation. He could not be friends with white children. He could not play in the same parks, or go to the same movie theaters.

King used his powerful voice to spread his message of equality.

DID YOU KNOW?

As a young student, King won a speaking contest. His speech was about ending segregation and treating all people equally.

In college, King studied Gandhi—the man who taught people peaceful ways to make India a better place.

King grew up wanting to change the way African Americans were treated. King worked hard in school. He wanted a job helping others. He decided to go to college to become a **minister**.

The Power of Peace

King believed segregation could be changed in a peaceful way. King organized marches, **sit-ins**, and **boycotts**. King gave speeches encouraging people to support equal rights for all Americans.

In 1963, King helped lead over 200,000 people on a march in Washington, DC.

DID YOU KNOW?

"I Have a Dream" is the name of King's most famous speech. In this speech, King shares his dream of living in a fair and peaceful world.

- This picture shows King giving his "I Have a Dream" speech to millions of people across the country.

Not everyone agreed with King's message. Some people did not believe African Americans should have the same rights as white people in the U.S. Some people tried to stop King from doing his work. They put him in jail. People even tried to hurt King and his family.

Important Changes

King's work helped make important changes in the U.S. In 1964, the U.S. government passed the Civil Rights Act. The Civil Rights Act ended segregation.

African American and white children could attend the same schools. They could play at the same playgrounds. African Americans had the same rights and freedoms as everyone in the U.S.

King met with President Lyndon B. Johnson when he signed the Civil Rights Act into law.

In 1964, King received the Nobel Peace Prize for his work. This award is a great achievement. Only one person in the world receives this award each year.

• King received the Nobel Peace Prize for his work in the civil rights movement.

DID YOU KNOW?

At the time, King was the youngest person to win the Nobel Peace Prize. He was 35 years old.

A Sad Day

On April 4, 1968, a man named James Earl Ray shot King. Ray was against African Americans having equal rights. King was 39 years old. He had a wife and four young children.

King's funeral was held at Ebenezer Baptist Church— where King was a minister.

DID YOU KNOW?

The idea of creating a national holiday to honor King was suggested just four days after his death.

U.S. President Barack Obama and members of King's family visit King's grave.

King's death shocked and saddened people around the world. Thousands of people came to King's funeral. People wanted to honor his memory. Even though King was gone, people wanted to continue his important work.

Creating the Holiday

It took many years for the government to make Martin Luther King, Jr. Day a holiday. It was hard work, but people across the country did not give up! In 1982, more than six million people signed a **petition** to show support of a holiday to honor King.

Cities all over the world have streets named in honor of Martin Luther King, Jr.

DID YOU KNOW?

Many cities have streets, buildings, or parks named after Martin Luther King, Jr. Do you have a place named after King where you live?

In 1983, U.S. President Ronald Reagan signed a law to create a holiday to honor King's important work. People celebrated the first Martin Luther King, Jr. Day on January 20, 1986.

King's family watches as President Reagan signs the law to create Martin Luther King, Jr. Day.

Celebrations

People celebrate Martin Luther King, Jr. Day in different ways. Many cities hold marches or parades to honor King's memory.

People from different backgrounds join together to march in King's honor.

DID YOU KNOW?

More than 100 countries around the world have a holiday to honor Martin Luther King, Jr.

This man is holding a sign to honor King's memory.

People come together to march for peace and equal rights. Some people carry signs with words to support King's message. The marches remind people of the many peaceful marches King led.

Services and Speeches

Some people attend special services at their churches on Martin Luther King, Jr. Day. These services celebrate King's strong **faith** and peaceful message. People pray for peace and give thanks for King's work.

This church choir honors King's memory through songs and music.

DID YOU KNOW?

King and his father both worked as ministers at Ebenezer Baptist Church in Atlanta, Georgia.

Many people sing King's favorite **hymns** and songs written to honor his memory. People also listen to recordings from some of his most famous speeches. His words encourage people to carry on his work.

A Martin Luther King, Jr. Day service honors King's memory at Ebenezer Baptist Church.

THE 2004 KING HOLIDAY OBSERVANCE
IN HONOR OF THE 75th BIRTHDAY OF
DR. MARTIN LUTHER KING, JR.

THE 36th ANNUAL
MARTIN LUTHER KING, JR.
COMMEMORATIVE SERVICE
JANUARY 19, 2004

Visiting Sites

People also celebrate Martin Luther King, Jr. Day by visiting places built in his honor. Many cities have **monuments** built to remember King. The monuments remind people of King's important work.

This picture shows a statue of Martin Luther King, Jr. in Riverside, California.

DID YOU KNOW?

The Martin Luther King, Jr. National Memorial is being built in Washington, DC.

The King Center in Atlanta, Georgia, is a place built to teach people about King's message. Each year more than 650,000 people from all over the world visit The King Center. People come to learn more about King's work and his message of peace.

These children visit The King Center on a class trip.

Learning King's Message

Many schools celebrate Martin Luther King, Jr. Day. Children learn about King's life and his work. Students are encouraged to spread King's message of love, equality, and peace.

This girl performs a speech to honor King's message.

DID YOU KNOW?

Some schools hold public speaking contests to honor King's message. Students write speeches about peace and equal rights. They perform the speeches in front of classmates.

Students memorize King's words from his famous speeches. Students also learn about the civil rights movement. Students are taught how King made the country a better place.

These children work together to create a poster to spread King's peaceful message.

Day of Service

In 1994, Congress named Martin Luther King, Jr. Day a national day of volunteer service. In 2008, more than half a million people across the country came together to help others.

These children are planting flowers to make their community a more beautiful place.

DID YOU KNOW?

In 2008, Philadelphia had more than 60,000 volunteers take part in the Day of Service.

Some people helped clean up their communities by picking up litter or fixing old houses. Other people planted flowers in city parks or brought food to the hungry. People of all ages can join in to help others in their communities.

These girls honor King by cleaning up their community.

Celebrate Every Day

Martin Luther King, Jr. worked to make the U.S. a better place for everyone. He helped earn equal rights for all Americans. He stood for equality and freedom. These are two important parts of U.S **culture**.

This painting celebrates how King's life inspired people.

DID YOU KNOW?

King is the only American other than George Washington to have a national holiday in honor of his birthday.

These people are helping others by collecting food to give to charity.

You can celebrate Martin Luther King, Jr. Day every day! You can do things to help people in your community. For example, you can give your old toys and clothing to **charity**. You can also honor King's memory by being kind to others and treating people fairly.

A King Quiz

Test your Martin Luther King, Jr. knowledge! Check your answers at the bottom of the next page.

1. Where was King born?
2. Who inspired King's message of non-violence?
3. What was Martin Luther King, Jr. job?
4. How did the 1964 Civil Rights Act help the civil rights movement?
5. When do we celebrate Martin Luther King, Jr. Day?

DID YOU KNOW?

You can listen to King's famous "I Have a Dream" speech at www.mlkonline.net/sounds.html

These children are learning about Martin Luther King, Jr. at school.

Answers:
1. Martin Luther King, Jr. was born in Atlanta, Georgia.
2. Gandhi inspired King's message of non-violence.
3. Martin Luther King, Jr. was a minister.
4. The Civil Rights Act ended segregation.
5. People celebrate Martin Luther King, Jr. Day on the third Monday in January.

Glossary

boycott To refuse to take part in something as a way of protesting

charity An organization that helps people in need

civil rights The rights of all people to equal treatment

culture The features of everyday life shared by people in a particular place

equality Being equal in regards to rights, laws, and opportunities

faith Belief and trust in God

federal Country-wide or national

honor To show respect for someone

hymn A song of praise

kidnap To take a person against his or her will

minister The leader of a church

monument A statue or building that honors a person or event

petition A written request made to people in power

right What the law says people can do

segregation The act of keeping people or groups apart

sit-in The act of sitting in a public place as a way of protesting

slave A person who is treated like property and forced to work without pay

Index

Printed in the U.S.A. - CG